HANDMADE CRAFTS

by children for children

The author of this book, Guadalupe Rodríguez, has been working with children in the Azulillo kindergarten in Santiago, Chile, for over eighteen years. Guadalupe, the teachers and the children from the kindergarten worked together using simple materials, recycled junk and natural objects to come up with the craft projects in this book. This process taught the children that everything around them has potential and can be used to create beautiful things.

Many of these projects are traditional to Chile and have been passed down through the generations. The projects are perfect for a child and adult to do together. The simple way in which they inspire the imagination will appeal to children all around the world. Children will take pride in creating their own objects, animals or people so that they can say they made their own play things. Whether at home or in the classroom, we hope that children have fun experimenting with and learning from the craft projects in this book.

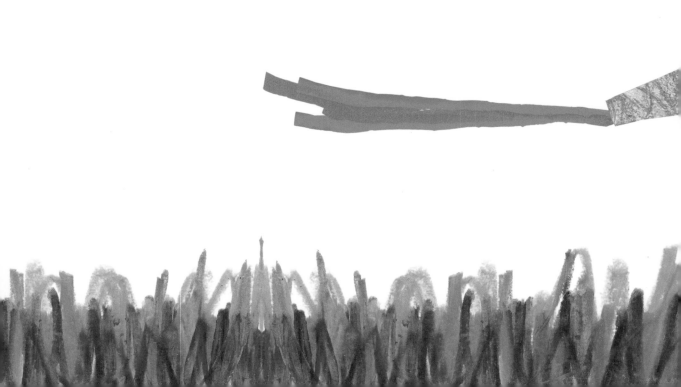

HANDMADE CRAFTS
by children for children

Guadalupe Rodríguez

translated from the original Spanish
by Catherine Bruzzone

b small publishing
www.bsmall.co.uk

CONTENTS

YOU WILL NEED

Keep a collection of useful junk. For example, you can use old cereal boxes for card, shopping bags often have cord handles, new clothes are packed in tissue paper, and so on. Here are the materials you will use in this book.

newspaper
plain paper
tracing paper
tissue paper
crêpe paper
card and cardboard boxes
egg boxes
twigs and sticks
clean ice-cream sticks
clean wooden kebab skewers
paper clips or pieces of wire

paper fasteners
scissors
craft glue
sticky tape
masking tape
pencils
wax crayons
paint
pastels
old material
string

wool
elastic or rubber bands
needle and thread
pegs
toilet roll and kitchen
   roll tubes
balloons
feathers
empty cotton reels
old broomstick
straws

(!)   Here you will need
        an adult to help you.

1   Open out a cardboard box (e.g. a cereal box) so that it lies flat.

2   Cut along the creases of the box to make parts of an animal or person. Look at the pictures to see the sort of shapes you will need. Then colour them.

3   Build your animal or person using paper fasteners.

6

ANIMALS
IN THE WILD

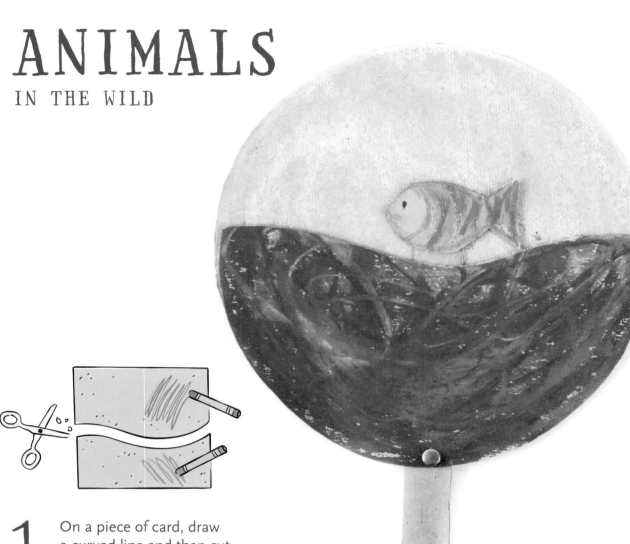

1 On a piece of card, draw a curved line and then cut along it. Colour one part the colour of the sky and the other like a field or the sea.

2 Glue the two pieces together but only use glue on the two edges. (You must be able to open up the centre.)

3 On another piece of card draw and colour in or paint an animal. Then cut it out. Cut a strip of card 30 x 3 centimetres. Glue one end of the strip of card to the back of the animal and wait until it has dried well.

4 Then push the card strip through the centre of the landscape and fix it with a paper fastener, as shown in the picture. You can make your little animal walk through the landscape by moving the piece of card backwards and forwards.

FLAT MASK

1 On a piece of card, mark a circle the same size as your face. If you are making an animal, add ears. Cut out the face and draw on whiskers, nose and ears. Cut holes for the eyes.

2 If you are making a person, draw the eyes and mouth. Cut them out and then colour on eyebrows, eyelashes, nose and cheeks.

3 On the back, glue on an ice-cream stick and wait for it to dry.

10

MASK

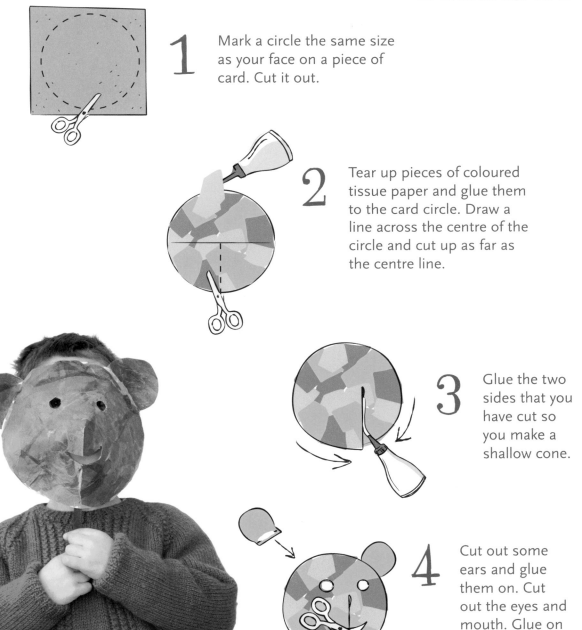

1 Mark a circle the same size as your face on a piece of card. Cut it out.

2 Tear up pieces of coloured tissue paper and glue them to the card circle. Draw a line across the centre of the circle and cut up as far as the centre line.

3 Glue the two sides that you have cut so you make a shallow cone.

4 Cut out some ears and glue them on. Cut out the eyes and mouth. Glue on an ice-cream stick, see page 10.

11

PEG
ANIMALS

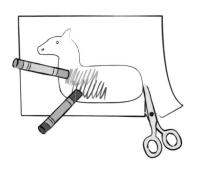

1 Draw the body of an animal on a piece of card, colour it and cut it out.

2 Glue a piece of string or wool for the tail. Then glue scraps of material for the ears.

3 Take two pegs and colour them to match the body of your animal. Glue them on to the body. Wait until it has dried well.

PEG
BUGS

1 Colour a peg with wax crayons or pastels.

2 On a piece of paper, draw and cut out the wings of your bug.

3 Then glue them on to the top of the peg. Cut and glue two or more little pieces of grass or twigs for antennae or legs for your bug. Wait until it has dried well.

PUPPET THEATRE

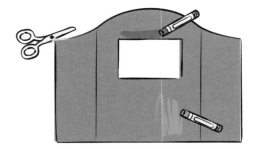

1 To make the puppets, scrunch up a small ball of newspaper and wrap it in a scrap of plain material. Insert a small stick or a twig and tie the material with a piece of string. Use another scrap of coloured material to dress the puppet and tie it at the neck. Colour the face and glue on pieces of wool for hair.

2 Open a large cardboard box and cut it the shape of a theatre. Then cut a rectangle in the middle as a window. Colour the theatre.

3 For the curtains, cut two rectangles of material. Fold over the top of each piece and ask an adult to help you sew the folds so you can thread a piece of string through them. Measure a piece of string so that it is a few centimetres wider than the theatre window. Thread the piece of string through both curtains.

4 Make a hole in both sides of the theatre window. Put each end of the string in one of the holes and knot the ends so that they don't come out.

Open the curtains and now you're ready for your puppets to perform!

CARDBOARD TUBE
DOLLS

1 Take a toilet roll tube and glue on scraps of paper or material so that it is completely covered.

2 For the head of the doll, crunch newspaper up into a ball to fit on the end of the tube and cover it with sticky tape.

3 Wrap the ball with a piece of plain material and tie it with string.

4 Using paper, pieces of old sock or material, make a hat for your doll. Glue it on.

5 Colour eyes, a nose and mouth on your doll. Glue the head on to the end of the tube.

ANIMALS

1 Scrunch a piece of newspaper up and wrap it with masking tape, shaping it into the body and head of an animal.

2 Using PVA glue mixed with a little water, cover your animal with pieces of coloured tissue paper. Leave it overnight so that it dries completely.

3 Using children's scissors, make two or four holes for the legs, depending on what sort of animal you're making. Glue little twigs into the holes. Leave to dry.

4 Cut out and glue on the ears, tail or any other details. Draw on the eyes.

20

MAGIC
BLACKBOARD

1 Take a piece of white paper and colour all over it using different coloured wax crayons.

2 Cover the colours completely with black poster paint or black crayon. (Wait until the paint is all dry.)

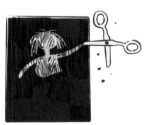

3 Using children's scissors, an opened paper clip, a pen lid or old, empty biro, scratch the shape of a person or animal. Watch the colours appear!

PAPER BIRDS

1 Use a plate to mark a circle on tracing paper or card. Cut it out and fold it in half.

2 Draw and then cut out tail feathers and a beak from tissue paper. Glue them on and paint an eye on each side of the paper or card. Choose two thin twigs for the legs and glue them on.

3 Ask an adult to help pass a needle and thread through your little bird to hang it up and... it's ready to fly away!

23

GIRLS AND BOYS

HOLDING HANDS

1   Cut a very long rectangle from card. Fold it like a concertina. All the folded pieces should be the same size.

2   Draw the shape of a boy or girl on the first fold. It's important that the arms and legs go right to the edge of the paper. Cut round the shape, through all the folds.

3   Open the paper and colour each figure. Glue an ice-cream stick on to the legs of the two end children. Leave to dry.

PAPER
FLOWERS

1 Take a sheet of tissue paper and cut out different size circles. Repeat this with different coloured paper.

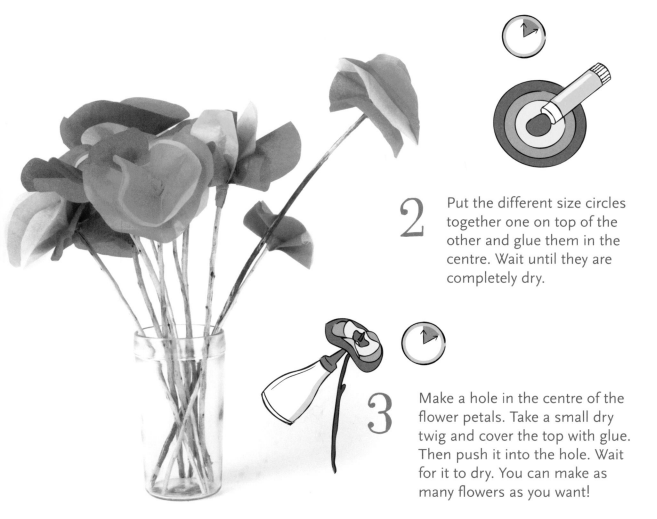

2 Put the different size circles together one on top of the other and glue them in the centre. Wait until they are completely dry.

3 Make a hole in the centre of the flower petals. Take a small dry twig and cover the top with glue. Then push it into the hole. Wait for it to dry. You can make as many flowers as you want!

POMPOMS

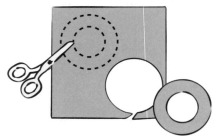

1 Draw two circles of the same size on a piece of card. Then draw another smaller circle inside each big circle. Cut them out.

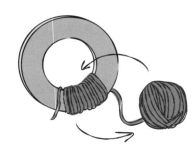

2 Put the two big circles together and begin to roll wool around them. Pass the wool through the hole. You can use different colour wool on the same pompom.

3 When the ring is completely covered with wool, put the point of your scissors between the two pieces of card and cut the wool along the edge, right round the circle. Ask an adult to help with this.

26

4 Pull the two card circles slightly apart and wind another piece of wool round the centre between the two pieces of card and knot it.

5 Take out the pieces of card and you have your pompom! To join two pompoms thread a needle with wool and push it through the centre of a pompom. Ask an adult to help you. Tie a knot to hold it in place and then push the needle through the second pompom. Tie a knot to secure it. You can join as many pompoms as you like.

6 To make eyes cut out some tiny circles of coloured card. Draw a black or brown dot in the middle. Glue on to the heads. Glue on coloured card for beaks or twigs for antennae.

PIÑATA

1 Inflate a balloon. Make a mixture of craft glue and water and use it to glue scraps of newspaper on to the balloon.

2 Cut and glue scraps of tissue paper on top of the newspaper. You can make eyes and a mouth or even some tentacles! Leave it to dry overnight.

3 Cut round the bottom of the dried shape. The balloon will burst. Then cut a large piece of crêpe paper and glue it inside the piñata. Leave to dry.

4 Glue a piece of string on top of the piñata so you can hang it up. Fill a paper bag with sweets and put it inside the piñata. Tie up the crêpe paper to close the piñata.

Have fun breaking the piñata to find the sweets!

FISH KITE

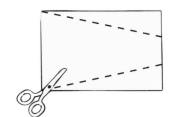 **1** On a piece of tracing paper, craft paper or any paper about 70 x 50 cm, draw two lines as shown on this picture. Cut out the shape.

 **2** Draw on the eyes and the body. Fold and glue the edges. Leave to dry.

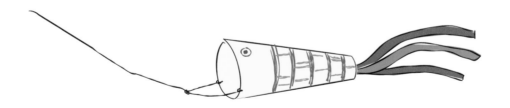

3 Make two holes and tie two lengths of string to the mouth end and knot them. Tie on a long piece of string to pull it. Glue paper strips for the tail.

PLASTIC BOTTLE
DOLLS

1 Scrunch up a ball of newspaper for the doll's head. Wrap it in plain cloth and tie this with string.

2 Push the bottom of the folded material into the mouth of the plastic bottle. Glue it in.

3 Wrap the bottle with pieces of cloth to look like your doll's clothes. Then draw on a face.

MASK

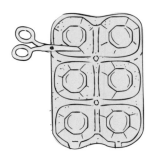

1 Take an egg box and cut off two egg spaces.

2 Cut a hole in the bottom of each space. Then glue some feathers on the top edge.

3 Glue an ice-cream stick or twig on to the bottom. Leave to dry. (You can paint your mask too.)

WOOLLEN DOLLS

1
Cut two different colour lengths of wool of 120 centimetres. Tie them with a knot. Then, using a door handle to help you, twist them together.

2
Fold your pieces of wool in half and they will twist in the other direction. Make a knot at each end. Now you have your first woollen twist ready. Repeat twice more so that you have three pieces of twisted wool.

3
On a piece of card, draw your doll's face. Then colour it and cut it out. Take a peg and glue the face to one end.

4
Put the top of the peg half way along one woollen twist. Roll it up from the centre but leave a few centimetres of wool at each end, for arms. Tie it with a knot.

5 Glue the second twist of wool to the first. Roll it all up from the middle to the ends. Make a knot to fix it. Finally roll the third twist of wool gluing it to the front. Roll it all up from the middle to the ends. Leave a few centimetres for the legs. Fix it with a knot.

MOUSETRAP

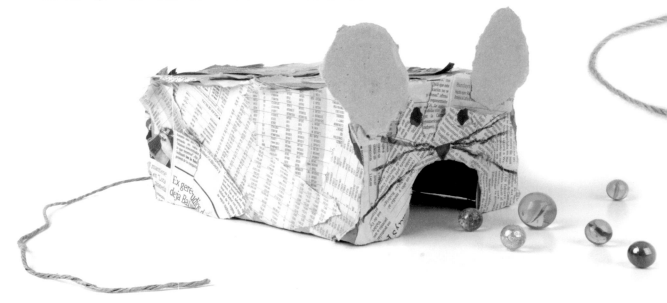

1   Cut a semi-circle on one side of a cardboard box. Glue on pieces of newspaper to cover it completely.

2   Draw two ears on a piece of grey card or paper and glue them on the box. When everything is dry, draw on the eyes and whiskers to make a mouse's face. Glue on a piece of string as a tail.

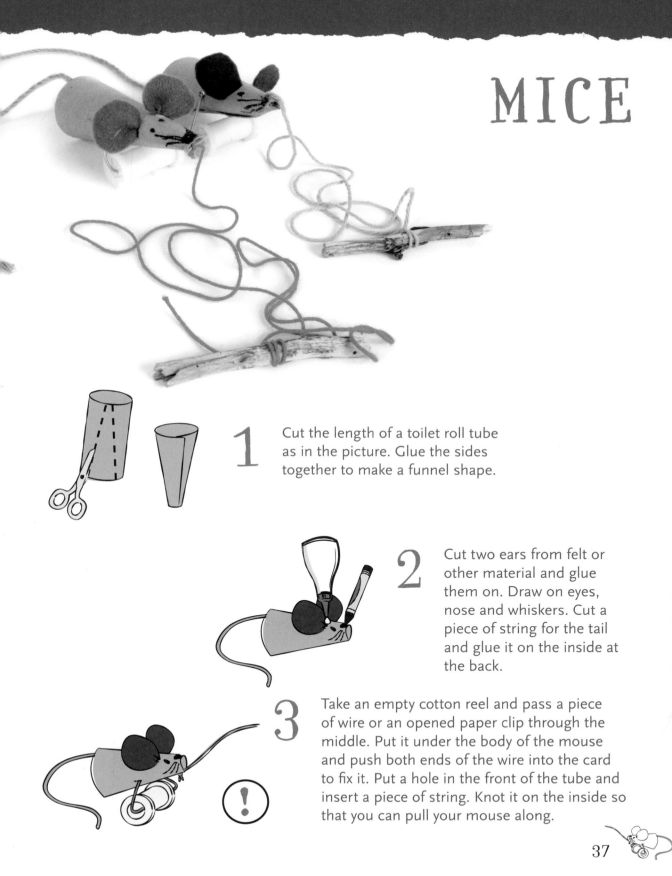

MICE

1 Cut the length of a toilet roll tube as in the picture. Glue the sides together to make a funnel shape.

2 Cut two ears from felt or other material and glue them on. Draw on eyes, nose and whiskers. Cut a piece of string for the tail and glue it on the inside at the back.

3 Take an empty cotton reel and pass a piece of wire or an opened paper clip through the middle. Put it under the body of the mouse and push both ends of the wire into the card to fix it. Put a hole in the front of the tube and insert a piece of string. Knot it on the inside so that you can pull your mouse along.

GIANT PAPER
BOAT

1 Glue together twelve sheets of newspaper by the edges then glue four half sheets down one side to make a gigantic square. Fold the square in half and then in half again to make a smaller square.

2 Position the square so that the folded edges are at the top and the separated edges are at the bottom (see picture to the left). Fold the first layer at the middle joining the bottom corner to the top corner. Fold the other three layers together the other way joining the bottom corners to the top corner on the other side. This will make a triangle.

3 Pull open the base of the triangle from the centre of each edge so that the two sharp corners move towards each other. It will look a bit like a huge bird's beak! Keep pulling gently until the corners meet. You will need to fold the paper so that it makes a diamond shape (see picture to the left). Pull the diamond shape open from the top (the closed end) like a flower opening until you have your gigantic boat.

ORGAN
GRINDER

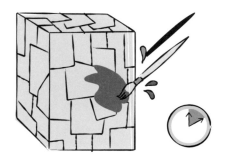

1 Glue pieces of newspaper all over a cardboard box to cover it. Wait until it dries well and then paint it.

2 Draw the slots and other details of the organ on to the painted box. Now insert a broomstick under the box and and tape it firmly in place.

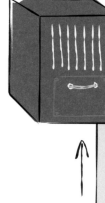

3 Make a handle with a paper clip or piece of wire. Cover it with masking tape and paint it. Leave it to dry and then fix it on to the organ with sticky tape.

4 Cut the length of a kitchen roll tube as shown in the picture. Glue the sides together to make a funnel shape. Then glue the funnel on top of the organ as in the picture.

5 Draw some pretty flags
and paint them. The flag in
the picture is the Chilean
flag but you can use any
flag. Cut out the flags
and glue a wooden kebab
skewer on each flag. Push
the little flags into the cone
on the top of your organ.

You can also add little balls, a parrot
and windmills on to your organ.
They are on pages 42, 43 and 44.

PARROT

IN ITS CAGE

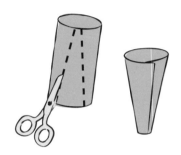

1 Cut the length of a toilet roll tube as in the picture. Glue the sides together to make a funnel shape.

2 Draw the parrot's feet and tail on the bottom of the cone and then cut them out.

3 Cut one egg space from an egg box. Glue it on as the parrot's head. From another piece of card, draw and cut out the parrot's beak. Glue it on to its head. Colour the parrot's body, face and eyes.

4 Take a cardboard box that is bigger than the parrot and paint it.

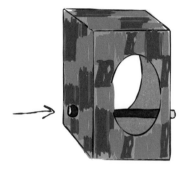

5 Cut two oval-shaped windows on opposite sides of the box. Push a stick through the other two sides of the box. Put your parrot in its cage. It is ready to go on the top of the organ on page 41.

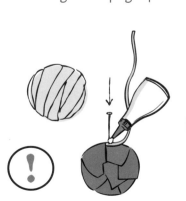

6 Make some balls to hang from the organ too. Scrunch up newspaper and cover with masking tape. Glue on pieces of coloured tissue paper. Ask an adult to help make a hole in the ball with a pin. Push in some glue and a long piece of elastic.

WINDMILL

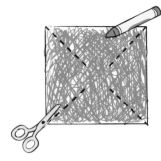

1 Cut a square of card and colour it on both sides. Draw two diagonal lines from one corner of the square to the opposite sides. Cut down the diagonal lines from the corners but stop 2 centimetres from the centre.

2 Fold four of the eight points to the centre, one after the other, and glue them on top of each other.

3 Take a stick and a paper clip. Open the paper clip and twist it round the stick. Stretch out the rest of the wire.

4 Take a straw and cut off two 1-centimetre pieces. Push the end of the wire through one of the pieces. Then push it through the centre of the windmill. Put the second piece of straw on the end and fold over the wire to fix it.

44

PUPPETS

1 Make a ball of newspaper and wrap it in a plain piece of material. Push a stick into it and tie it with a piece of string. Draw a face on your ball and glue on a piece of material for a hat.

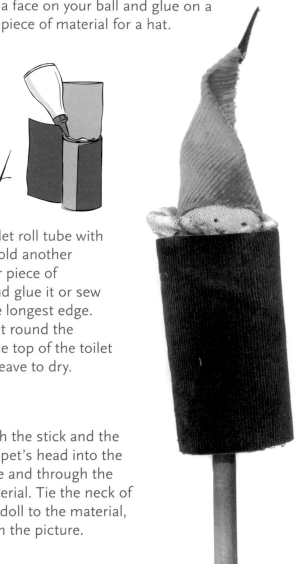

2 Cover a toilet roll tube with material. Fold another rectangular piece of material and glue it or sew it along the longest edge. Then glue it round the inside of the top of the toilet roll tube. Leave to dry.

3 Push the stick and the puppet's head into the tube and through the material. Tie the neck of the doll to the material, as in the picture.

Hold the puppet's stick and push it up and down so that its face appears and disappears.

45

CARDBOARD TUBE
BEARS

1 Cut a toilet roll tube into the shape of a bear's body and back paws. Cut front paws out of another tube, as shown in the picture.

2 Cut one egg space from an egg box but leave two points for ears.

3 Glue the head and arms on to the bear. Paint the body and the face.

46